CW01654624

20 ESSENTIAL EXERCISES FOR BIGGER BICEPS

Quickly build big biceps with targeted weightlifting programs

JASON CURTIS

FUNDAMENTAL CHANGES

20 Essential Exercises for Bigger Biceps

Quickly build big biceps with targeted weightlifting programs

Published by **www.fundamental-lifestyle.com**

ISBN: 978-1-911267-84-3

www.fundamental-lifestyle.com

For more information about the author:

Website: **www.5sfitness.co.uk**

Facebook: **www.facebook.com/5sfitnessuk**

Instagram: **www.instagram.com/5s_fitness**

Twitter: **www.twitter.com/5sfitness**

YouTube: **http://bit.ly/2GksRK1**

Other Books from Fundamental Lifestyle

Fix Your Posture – The Simple Exercise Solution

Free Yourself from Aches and Pains Caused by Bad Posture

- Discover simple, yet life-changing posture correcting exercises and techniques.
- Understand how to fix your seated, standing and sleeping posture and reduce aches and pains.
- Build healthy posture habits that will have you living pain free.
- Stop allowing poor posture and pain to put your life on hold!
- Eliminate pain and discomfort in your neck, back, shoulders, hips and legs.

Strength and Mobility Exercises for Runners

Improve your Running Speed, Mobility and Strength

- Simple, effective exercises and example programs to follow
- Understand how to build strength, speed and mobility to become a better runner
- Build healthy training habits that will drastically improve and lengthen your running career
- Learn to boost your endurance, while preventing injury
- Over 50 exercises with clear photos and instructions, so each exercise can be completed confidently and correctly

Contents

Other Books from Fundamental Lifestyle 3

Introduction 7
Get the Videos 7
Anatomy of the Biceps 9
The Biceps Group 10
The Biceps Group 11
Equipment 12

Chapter One: Compound Movements 13
Supinated Bent Over Rows 14
Batwing Rows 15
Single Arm Rows 16
Chin Ups 17
V-Grip Pull Ups 18
Inverted Rows 19

Chapter Two: Barbell & EZ Bar 21
Introduction 21
Standing Barbell Curls 22
Standing EZ Bar Curls 23
Reverse Barbell/EZ Bar Curls 24
Barbell/EZ Bar Drag Curl 25
EZ Preacher Curls 26

Chapter Three: Dumbbells 27
Introduction 27
Full Dumbbell Curls 28
Hammer Curls 29
Cross-Body Hammer Curls 30
Zottman Curls 31
Incline Bench Curls 32
Spider Curls 33
Concentration Curls 34
Dumbbell Preacher Curl 35

Chapter Four: Biceps Prehab 37
Introduction 37
Resistance Band Curls 38
Massage Ball Biceps Release 39
Barbell Biceps Release Technique 40
Biceps Wall Stretch 41

Chapter Five: Programming 43
Introduction 43
Pull Workout 1: 44
Pull Workout 2: 44
Pull Workout 3: 44
Dumbbell Super-Set: 45
Dumbbell Tri-Set: 45
Dumbbell Giant-Set: 45

Bonus Content: Fix Your Posture 47
Introduction 47
Standing Posture 47
Head Retractions & Scapula Pinches 48
Head Retractions: 48
Scapula Pinches: 49
Shoulder External Rotation 50
External Rotations – Long Band: 51
External Rotations – Small Loop Band: 52
Serratus Wall Slides 53
Serratus Wall Slides – Foam Roller: 54
Band Pull Apart 55
Standard Pull Apart: 55
Star Pattern: 56
Extra Drill – Band Front-to-Backs: 57
Band Face Pulls 58
Band Horizontal Pulls 59
Bilateral: 59
Unilateral: 60

Glossary of Terms and Equipment 61

Introduction

The biceps have become an iconic symbol of the gym body, with males generally wanting to gain big arms, and females wanting to develop lean, athletic arms.

Although the biceps are highly valued when it comes to aesthetics, specifically targeting the biceps is often frowned upon by functional fitness experts who place high value on total body (compound) movements. However, this holistic approach doesn't mean we should neglect single joint actions. If there is time (after the compound lifts), it makes sense to target specific areas.

This book teaches you why the biceps are an important muscle group, and shows you the most effective ways to train them.

When working the biceps, a lot of effort tends to be focused into the forward direction. This can have a detrimental effect on your posture, leading to rounded shoulders and a forward head position. To help counteract this effect, I have included some important and helpful exercises from my book, *Fix Your Posture*. You should work these exercises into your programming at least twice a week.

Get the Videos

The videos to accompany each exercise are available to download for free from

http://geni.us/bicepsvideos

Simply enrol in the course and you'll have free access to all 16 videos.

If you type above link into a browser, please note that there is no "www."

You can also scan the QR code below to view the videos on your smartphone:

Anatomy of the Biceps

The biceps, or *biceps brachii*, is a two-headed muscle (hence *Bi*) on the front of your upper arm.

The Biceps

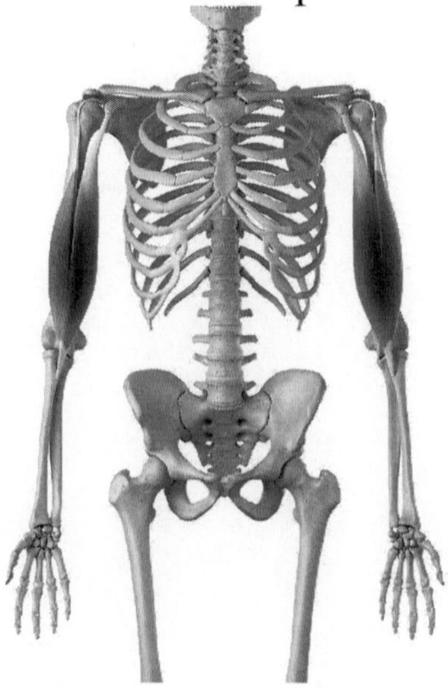

The *belly* of a muscle is the central bulging portion (the bit you squeeze when you tense your biceps), and the heads of the muscle are its fixed point of origin.

The biceps have two heads (long and short), both of which attach high up in the shoulder on the scapula (shoulder blades). This means that the biceps play a small role in shoulder flexion (raising the arm forwards and upwards), and can be the cause of anterior (front) shoulder pain.

The biceps also cross the elbow joints and insert on the *radius* (forearm bone). Therefore, the biceps work to flex your elbow, which is its primary action.

The biceps insertion point below the elbow can be a common area of tendinopathy (a term used to describe various tendon ailments, such as tendonitis). Therefore, care must be taken not to overstress or tear this tendon.

The final action of the *biceps brachii*, is supination of the forearm (turning the palms upwards) when the elbow is flexed. To see this in action, bend your elbows at 90 degrees, rotate your forearm back and forth and you will see your biceps moving.

The above actions must be considered when incorporating biceps exercises into our workouts. However, there are also other muscles that make up the *biceps group*. This group by no means includes all the muscles that cross the anterior side of your shoulder and elbow, but will include the ones that are notable for this book.

The Biceps Group

The Short Head of the *Biceps Brachii*

This part of the *biceps brachii* is best targeted by using a supinated (underhand) grip, with your hands in front of your body.

The Short Head of the Biceps Brachii

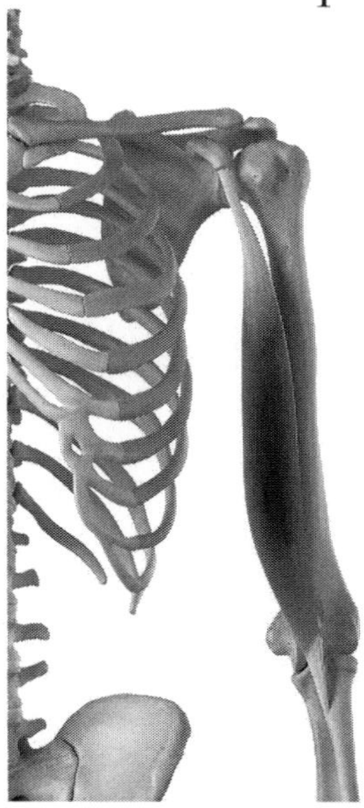

The Long Head of the Biceps Brachii

This part of the *biceps brachii* is best targeted when the arms are stretched back behind the body. For example, during an incline bench curl

The Long Head of the Biceps Brachii

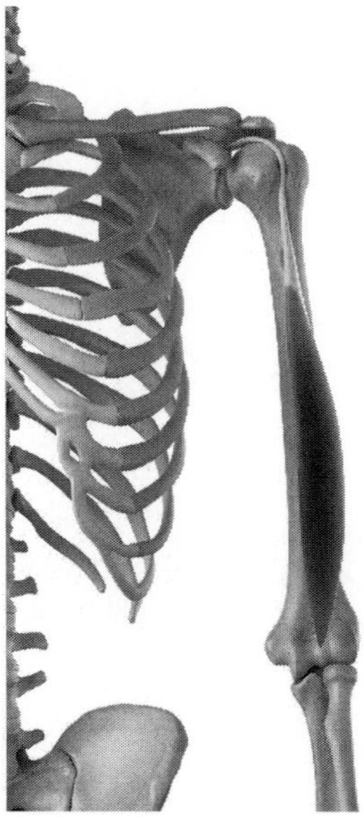

The Biceps Group

The *Brachialis*

This muscle lies deeper than the *biceps brachii* and helps to flex the elbow. The brachialis is best targeted by using a neutral grip (with the palms facing in).

The Brachialis

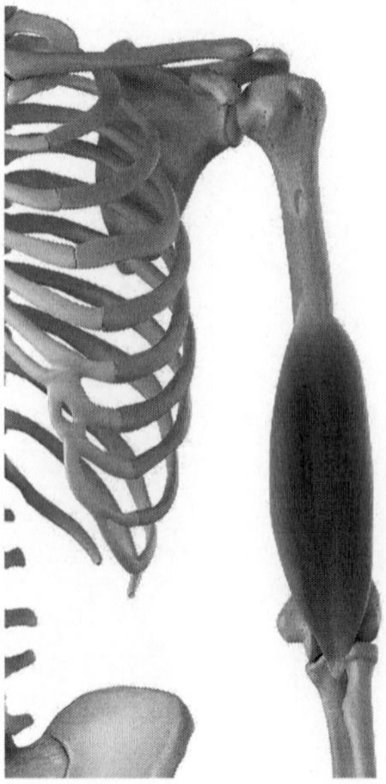

The *Brachioradialis*

This is the biggest muscle of your forearm and helps to flex the elbow. The *brachioradialis* is best targeted when using a pronated (overhand) grip, performing a reverse curl.

The Brachioradialis

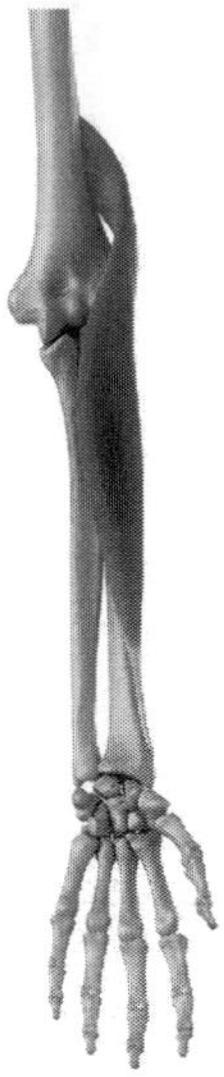

We don't need to isolate specific areas of the biceps group; this information simply helps us shift emphasis to a specific area. This is not only beneficial for muscular development, but also reduces the risk of repetitive strain injuries.

Repetitive strain injuries occur as a result of repetitive movements and overuse. Therefore, varying the way you work the biceps, and building these exercises around multi-joint (compound) exercises, is the key to keeping your joints healthy. This is explained further in Chapter One.

Equipment

Resistance machines and cables can be used to effectively train your biceps. However, this book deals with free weight equipment, specifically the barbell, the EZ bar, and dumbbells.

The barbell is the most efficient tool for total strength development. You can squat, push and pull (three of the major strength movements) a barbell and increase the weight over time to progressively load your muscles. This is the key to any decent strength training program.

It makes sense to combine compound and pull movements with single joint exercises using the barbell, EZ bar and dumbbells. This produces optimal workouts for both strength and *hypertrophy* (muscle building).

Resistance bands are a great bit of kit that can be used to get your biceps warmed up, create a huge pump, and keep your elbows in good health.

The equipment you'll need to access for this book is shown below.

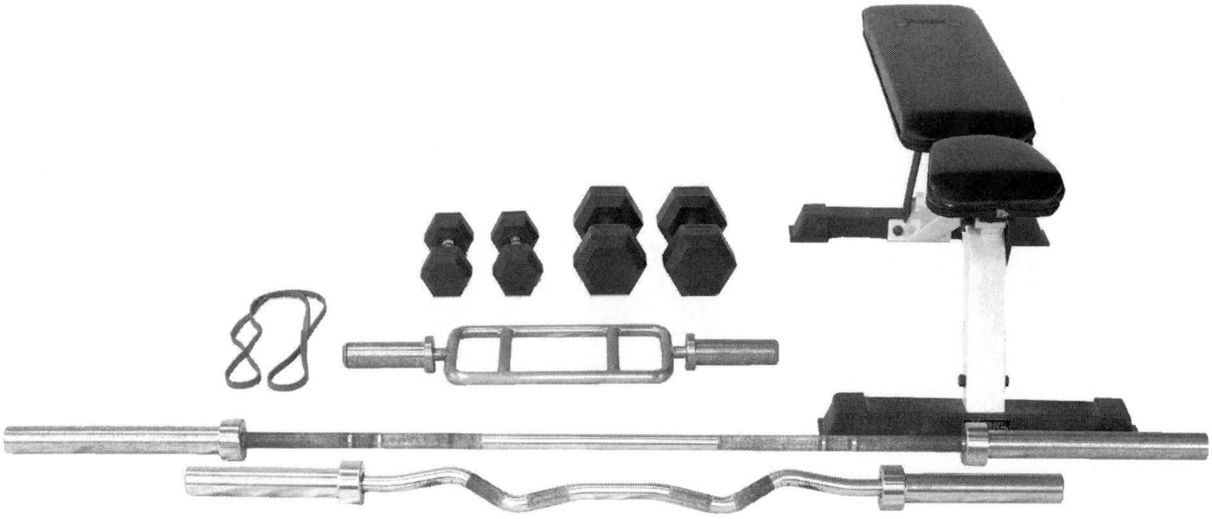

Chapter One: Compound Movements

The best way to program your training is to start with larger movements that work more muscle mass, and cause you to shift more weight.

It makes no sense to fatigue your forearms prior to performing a bent over row or a biceps curl. This is because your pre-fatigued forearms will hinder your ability to hold onto the barbell or dumbbells and limit the work you can achieve.

Pre-fatigue techniques (where you pre-work a muscle prior to the main workout) can be useful if you are trying to overload a specific muscle. However, I will not be including these techniques in this book because they have limited use in this context.

Beginning your workout with compound pulling actions that incorporate your biceps will *potentiate* your muscle fibres. Potentiation, in this context, is an increase of strength in the nerve pathways that have been used in a previous exercise. In layman's terms, this means that the associated muscles are primed and working at full capacity.

For example, when you pick up a light object up after lifting a much heavier weight, the lighter weight somehow feels almost abnormally easy. In the same way, performing heavy rows (for example) prior to doing biceps curls, makes for an optimal session, both physiologically and psychologically.

Remember, compound exercises are also an important part of reducing the risk of these ailments.

Single-joint actions are often incredibly stressful on the joint. When holding a dumbbell in your hand with your elbow bent at 90 degrees, your forearm is essentially a lever. This is not a biomechanically efficient position, as your biceps must produce 150kg (330 lbs) of force just to curl a 10kg (22lb) dumbbell. It is easy to see why spending whole sessions working on single joint actions can quickly lead to injuries.

Instead, you should begin your session with compound movements that spread stress across various structures, before finishing with a few single-joint exercises.

Finally, an important concept is the Mind-Muscle connection. This is consciously thinking about the muscle you are working to increase its engagement. Mind-Muscle connection should be applied to exercises in this book.

Don't forget: The videos to accompany each exercise are available to download for free from

http://geni.us/bicepsvideos

Simply enrol in the course and you'll get free access to all 16 videos. If you type above link into a browser, please note that there is no "www." Alternatively, you can also scan the QR code below to view the videos on your smartphone:

Supinated Bent Over Rows

The bent over row is an important exercise that works the musculature of your back and your biceps.

A pronated grip (with the palms facing down or "overhand grip") is often used for barbell rows as this is the grip most commonly used with other barbell exercises. However, a supinated grip (palms facing up or "underhand" grip) will place more emphasis on your biceps, so the EZ bar is often used to increase comfort on the wrists.

When working out how much weight to use, begin with 1-2 warm-up sets to get a feel for the movement. Then, select a weight that will have you struggling on the last 2 or 3 reps.

1. Pick the barbell/EZ bar up with a supinated grip, ensuring you use proper technique to do so.
2. Hinge at your hips by pushing your glutes (buttocks) back and allowing your torso to drop forward.
3. As you hinge, bend your knees slightly to bring the barbell to your knees (or slightly below depending on limb lengths).
4. Your back position should be midway between straight up and parallel to the floor; around 45-60 degrees (see picture).
5. Pull the barbell up to just above your navel and control it as it lowers back down to the starting position. Allow your shoulders to protract slightly at the bottom to stretch the muscles of your back.
6. Complete 3-5 sets of 5-10 reps.

Batwing Rows

When performing bent over rows or bicep curls, it is easy to cheat the movement by "jerking" the weight upwards.

Having a slight jerking action when lifting heavy weight is not always a terrible thing, sometimes we simply want to move a heavy weight from point A to B to build strength. However, if the aim is to target specific muscles, then smooth actions should be used.

The batwing row is a simple exercise that stops you using a jerking action by having you lay flat on a bench.

1. Lay chest first onto a flat or incline bench. The higher the incline, the more the upper back will be engaged.
2. If the bench is flat, you will most likely have to raise the bench up on platforms or plates.
3. Grab a dumbbell in each hand and allow your shoulders to protract (drop forward), to stretch the musculature of your back.
4. Pull the dumbbells upwards. This is usually done with a neutral grip so the dumbbells can come up to either side of the bench. However, a supinated grip can be used to increase the engagement of the biceps.
5. Complete 3-5 sets of 10-20 reps.

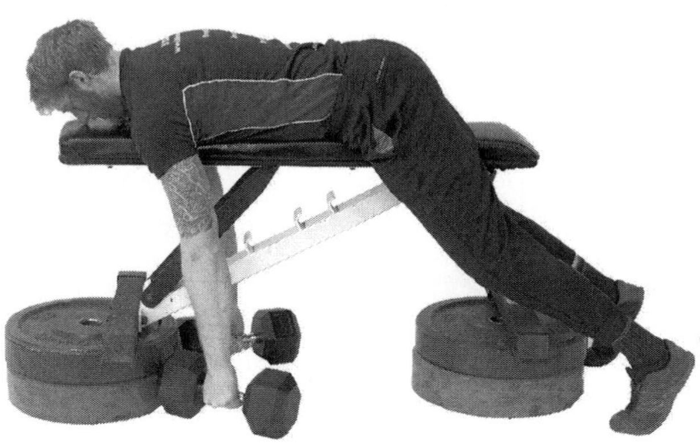

Single Arm Rows

Bilateral movements work both sides of the body simultaneously and are integral for strength development. However, unilateral exercises such as the single arm row also have many benefits.

Using a single dumbbell allows you to facilitate more rotation through your upper back during the row. This in turn allows a greater stretch on your lats and rhomboids (back muscles) and maximises the range of motion to increase the intensity of the exercise.

1. Single arm rows can be done with the knee and hand supported on a bench, or with just one hand on a bench as support. I prefer a single hand support.
2. For a single hand supported row, hinge at your hips and bend your knees slightly, placing your right hand on the bench.
3. Your feet should be slightly-wider-than-shoulder-width apart, either side by side or in a split stance where the same leg of the arm rowing is behind you.
4. Rows can be done with your torso parallel to the floor, although if your shoulders are slightly higher than your hips you will increase the engagement of your upper back.
5. Bend your knees to pick up the dumbbell before raising it 5-10 inches off the floor.
6. Pull the dumbbell up to your side while consciously engaging your back and rear delts to retract your shoulders. Pull hard with your biceps.
7. Lower the dumbbell gently and allow your shoulders to protract slightly to stretch the muscles of your back.
8. Complete 3-5 sets of 8-20 reps on each side.

Chin Ups

The term *pull ups* refers to pulling yourself up on a bar using a pronated grip. *Chin ups*, on the other hand, involve the same action but with a supinated grip. Chin ups greatly increase biceps engagement while also working your lats.

1. Grab the pull up bar with a supinated grip.

2. As you take your weight, brace your core and push your feet forward slightly to take them off the floor. This position keeps your pelvis in a neutral position. Keeping your knees bent with your feet to the rear disengages your core and can result in your pelvis tilting forward which can cause lower back pain.

3. Keep your shoulder blades pulled back so the musculature is engaged. Don't hang as a dead weight from your shoulders.

4. Use mind-muscle connection to ensure maximal engagement of your lats and biceps.

5. Pull hard with your back and biceps to bring your chin over, or your chest up to the bar.

6. Lower yourself down under control and return to the same posture as described in point 3.

7. Complete 3-5 sets of 2-10 reps.

V-Grip Pull Ups

This pull up variation uses a v-bar grip to vary the movement and increase the engagement of the biceps.

1. Place a V-grip over a pull up bar.
2. Grab either side of the V-grip.
3. As you take your weight, brace your core and push your feet forward slightly to take them off the floor.
4. As you pull yourself up, tilt your head to one side of the pull up bar and allow your shoulder to come up to the bar.
5. Lower back down under control, keeping tension in your back at the bottom, before raising back up, this time to the other side.
6. Complete 3-5 sets of 2-10 reps on each side.

Inverted Rows

Inverted rows can be performed well on a suspension trainer, however they are best done with a barbell and a rack.

1. Set a barbell up on a rack at mid-upper thigh height. Use spotter bars or pins so the barbell is secure.
2. Lay underneath the barbell and grab it with a pronated or supinated grip. Using a supinated grip will increase biceps engagement.
3. Bend your knees so that your feet are flat on the floor.
4. Squeeze your glutes to extend your hips and brace your core.
5. Raise yourself up so your lower chest touches the barbell.
6. Lower back down under control.
7. To increase the intensity of the exercise, elevate your feet off the floor with a couple of heavy plates.
8. Complete 3-5 sets of 5-20 reps.

Chapter Two: Barbell & EZ Bar

Introduction

When you have completed the compound pull movements it's now beneficial to use the barbell and EZ bar to perform exercises that isolate your biceps.

The barbell is a great tool for working the biceps. However, due to elbow/wrist anatomy and possible previous injuries, it can be quite stressful to hold a straight barbell with a supinated grip.

This is where the EZ bar comes into play. The curved grips of the bar allow you to hold it in positions that are much less stressful on your elbows and wrists. The only downside is that the EZ bar leaves your palms in a semi-supinated position which can restrict the biceps engagement you achieve at the top of the lift.

There are pros and cons to both the barbell and the EZ bar. The key is to find what works effectively for you, and mix up the exercises to get a total workout.

The first four exercises in this chapter are performed in a standing position. Although you don't want to cheat the isolation movement with too much leg drive or jerking, you can drive your legs into the floor to create momentum to get heavier weights moving.

Lighter loads are usually used during more specific single-joint exercises, to really isolate the muscles.

Standing Barbell Curls

The barbell curl puts emphasis on the *biceps brachii* and is often seen as the king of biceps exercises because you can lift much greater weight on a barbell compared to a dumbbell.

When performing bicep curls in a standing position, it is essential to maintain good upper body posture. Pull your shoulders back, keep your chest proud and pull your chin upwards and rearwards.

Good posture ensures that stresses are placed evenly through the intended structures.

When working with a barbell or EZ bar, you can vary your grip width to target different parts of the biceps. A narrower-than-shoulder-width grip will place emphasis on the long head, a shoulder-width / slightly-wider-than-shoulder-width grip will place emphasis on the short head.

1. Grab the barbell with a supinated grip.

2. Stand tall with good posture.

3. Contract your biceps to flex your elbows, bringing the barbell up towards your chest.

4. As your elbows pass 90 degrees of flexion, bring them forward slightly to increase the engagement of your biceps as you reach the top of the lift.

5. Lower the barbell back down to the starting position under control.

6. Complete 3-5 sets of 10 reps.

Standing EZ Bar Curls

EZ bar curls are an awesome variation to the barbell curl and apply much less stress to your wrists and elbows. This means that the EZ bar is an ideal tool to use when varying the width of your grip.

EZ bar curls put most emphasis on the *biceps brachii.*

1. Grab the EZ bar with a supinated grip.

2. Stand tall with good posture.

3. Contract your biceps to flex your elbows, bringing the bar up towards your chest.

4. As your elbows pass 90 degrees of flexion, bring them forward slightly to increase the engagement of your biceps as you reach the top of the lift.

5. Lower the EZ bar back down to the starting position under control.

6. Complete 3-5 sets of 10 reps.

Reverse Barbell/EZ Bar Curls

This curl variation can be done with the barbell or the EZ bar. However, the barbell will keep you in a fully pronated position throughout the curl.

This exercise will place most emphasis on your *brachioradialis*.

1. Grab the barbell or EZ bar with a pronated grip.

2. Stand tall with good posture.

3. Contract your biceps to flex your elbows and bring the barbell up towards your chest.

4. Lower the barbell back down to the starting position under control.

5. Complete 3-5 sets of 10 reps.

Barbell/EZ Bar Drag Curl

The drag curl can be performed with a barbell or EZ bar. As your elbows bend, the bar maintains contact with your torso.

This exercise places most emphasis on the *biceps brachii.*

1. Start with the bar in a standing curl position.

2. Keep your elbows rearwards and pull the bar up your torso.

3. Maintain contact with your torso until your elbows are fully bent to the rear.

4. Lower the bar back to the starting position. Again, maintain contact with your torso throughout.

5. Complete 3-5 sets of 10 reps.

EZ Preacher Curls

Preacher curls should be performed on a preacher curl bench. However, if a preacher curl bench isn't available you can improvise with an incline bench covered with a thick mat. They are most often performed with an EZ bar for comfort and ease of setup.

This exercise places most emphasis on the *biceps brachii.*

1. Grab the EZ bar with a supinated grip and place the backs of your arms over the bench.
2. Lower the bar down under control until your elbows are fully extended. Be cautious as this exercise often places an intense stretch on your biceps.
3. Contract your biceps and raise the bar back up towards your face.
4. Complete 3-5 sets of 10 reps.

Chapter Three: Dumbbells

Introduction

For specific biceps development, dumbbells are the most versatile piece of equipment in the gym. You can use them to incorporate all three actions of the biceps while you perform a single curl: flex the elbow, supinate the forearm and flex the shoulder.

You can work with dumbbells *unilaterally* (one arm at a time) and *bilaterally* (both arms at the same time). One of the benefits of working unilaterally is that you can place more emphasis on the targeted biceps and have greater focus on your mind-muscle connection.

When working unilaterally on a single-joint action, your neuromuscular system can place all its efforts on contracting and stabilising one side. Therefore, you will usually lift heavier with a unilateral, rather than bilateral curl.

Full Dumbbell Curls

I refer to this exercise as a *full curl* as it works all three actions of the biceps during each rep. This is something you can't do with a barbell or EZ bar.

This exercise can be performed unilaterally or bilaterally.

1. Stand tall with good posture.
2. Hold the dumbbells at your side in a neutral grip – starting in a neutral grip allows you to supinate your forearms as you perform the curl, helping to increase biceps engagement.
3. Contract your biceps, bringing the dumbbells upwards. As this happens, begin to supinate your forearms.
4. As your elbows pass 90 degrees of flexion, bring your elbows forward slightly to increase the engagement of your biceps as you reach the top of the lift.
5. As you get to the top of the lift, supinate your palms as hard as you can to increase the engagement of the biceps – push your little fingers in towards your chest.
6. A shift grip (pictured) can be used to increase the work required to supinate your forearms.
7. Lower the dumbbells down under control to the starting position.
8. Don't swing the dumbbells rearwards.
9. Complete 3-5 sets of 10 reps.

Hammer Curls

The next two exercises increase the engagement of the *brachialis*.

The *brachialis* lies deeper than the biceps brachii, and when trained, can increase the width/thickness of your arms.

This exercise can be performed unilaterally or bilaterally.

1. Stand tall with good posture.
2. Hold the dumbbells at your side with a neutral grip.
3. Contract your biceps to bring the dumbbells upwards.
4. Keep your hands in the neutral position.
5. As your elbows pass 90 degrees of flexion, bring your elbows forward slightly to increase the engagement of your biceps as you reach the top of the lift.
6. The top bell of the dumbbells should come up towards, or slightly above your shoulders. Squeeze your biceps hard at the top.
7. Lower the dumbbells down under control to the starting position.
8. Do not allow the dumbbell to swing rearwards.
9. Complete 3-5 sets of 10 reps.

Cross-Body Hammer Curls

Just like conventional hammer curls, the cross-body variant places most emphasis on the *brachialis*.

This exercise allows you to work with heavier dumbbells. Therefore, I often use it at the start of dumbbell workouts (often with higher reps) to get a great pump on the *brachialis*.

This exercise is performed unilaterally.

1. Stand tall with good posture.
2. Hold the dumbbells at your side in a neutral grip.
3. Contract your biceps, bringing one dumbbell upwards and across your body.
4. Keep your hands in the neutral position (palms facing your body throughout).
5. Bring the dumbbell up towards your *sternum* (breastbone).
6. Lower the dumbbell down under control to the starting position and work the opposite side.
7. Avoid using a jerking action to throw the dumbbells up.
8. Complete 3-5 sets of 10 reps.

Zottman Curls

These curls are named after George Zottman, a strongman in the 1800s.

The curl consists of a full dumbbell curl, the rotation of your forearms to face your palms forwards, and the lowering of the dumbbell in a reverse curl position.

This exercise can be performed unilaterally or bilaterally.

1. Stand tall with good posture.
2. Hold the dumbbells at your side in a neutral grip.
3. Contract your biceps to bring the dumbbells upwards. As this happens, turn your palms upwards to supinate your forearms.
4. As your elbows pass 90 degrees of flexion, bring your elbows forward slightly to increase the engagement of your biceps as you reach the top of the lift.
5. As you get to the top of the lift, squeeze your palms as hard as you can to increase the engagement of the biceps – push your little fingers in towards your chest.
6. At the top, rotate your wrists round so that your palms are facing forwards.
7. Lower the dumbbells down in a reverse curl position.
8. Don't allow the dumbbell to swing rearwards.
9. Complete 3-5 sets of 10 reps.

Incline Bench Curls

An incline bench can be used effectively with many dumbbell curl variations.

Laying on an incline bench allows you to hold the dumbbells behind your body. This creates a greater stretch on the *biceps brachii,* specifically in the long head.

This exercise can be performed unilaterally or bilaterally.

1. Lay on an incline bench.
2. With a dumbbell in each hand, allow your arms to drop straight down.
3. You can start with a supinated grip (palms forward), or start with a neutral grip to benefit from supinating the palms as you curl. Experiment to discover what works best for you.
4. Contract your biceps and raise the dumbbells up.
5. Slowly lower the dumbbells under control and allow for a full stretch on your biceps.
6. Do not allow the dumbbell to swing rearwards.
7. Complete 3-5 sets of 10 reps.

Spider Curls

This curl variation often uses a barbell or EZ bar. However, I have included it here with the incline bench curls, as spider curls also utilise an incline bench, and can be worked well with dumbbells.

1. Lay chest down on a high incline bench.
2. With a dumbbell in each hand, allow your arms to drop straight down. Your arms will fall in front of your body rather than behind as they do during an incline bench curl.
3. Start with your hands in a supinated position However, you can also use a neutral grip for hammer curls or when using the *full curl* technique.
4. Contract your biceps and raise the dumbbells up to the top position of the variant you are doing.
5. Slowly lower the dumbbells under control and allow for a full stretch on your biceps.
6. Do not allow the dumbbell to swing rearwards.
7. Complete 3-5 sets of 10 reps.

Concentration Curls

Concentration curls are a unilateral exercise that target the *biceps brachii.*

The setup of this exercise, along with mind-muscle connection (you can literally stare at your muscle as it contracts) makes the concentration curl one of the best isolation exercises for your biceps.

1. Sit on a flat bench with your feet flat on the floor and your knees spread.

2. Pick up a dumbbell with your right hand and place the back of your right arm on the inner thigh of your right leg. Ensure your biceps are facing directly away from your thigh.

3. Support yourself with your left hand on your left thigh.

4. At this point, your arm should be extended with the dumbbell off the floor.

5. While keeping your torso and upper arm completely still, contract your biceps and curl the dumbbell up towards your right shoulder. Squeeze your biceps hard at the top.

6. Slowly lower the dumbbell under control.

7. Complete 3-5 sets of 10 reps on each side.

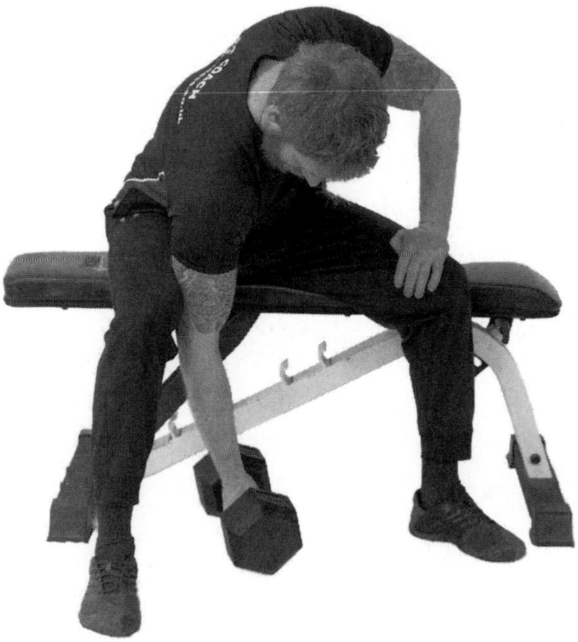

Dumbbell Preacher Curl

I have already shown you how to perform a preacher curl with an EZ bar. The last exercise of this chapter is the dumbbell unilateral variant.

Use a preacher curl bench, or an incline bench as shown in the picture.

This exercise places most emphasis on the *biceps brachii.*

1. Grab a dumbbell and place the back of your arm over the bench.

2. Support yourself with your other arm.

5. Lower the dumbbell down under control until your elbow is fully extended. Be cautious as this exercise often places an intense stretch on your biceps.

3. Contract your biceps and raise the dumbbell back up towards your face.

4. Complete 3-5 sets of 10 reps on each side.

Chapter Four: Biceps Prehab

Introduction

The biceps often get a lot of attention in the gym. However, the biceps are often left out when it comes to release techniques and stretches.

Release techniques are a hands-on type of therapy that can be performed yourself, usually with a foam roller or massage ball. The aim is to use pressure to stimulate a sensory receptor called the *Golgi tendon organ* that tells the muscle fibres to relax.

These techniques will not stimulate a long-term change in muscle tension by themselves. Instead they will cause a short-term release of muscle tension, which in turn allows you to achieve a more effective stretch in the tissues.

Resistance Band Curls

Prior to performing any release techniques and stretches, I like to get a muscle working and warm so that it is much more malleable.

This drill uses a resistance band to get the biceps warm. Resistance bands are an awesome bit of kit that can get muscles working hard, yet minimise the stress placed on surrounding structures.

1. Use a red resistance band for warm up drills.
2. Grab the band in both hands and place one end of the band under the arches of both feet. Moving your feet wider will increase the band tension.
3. The band could also be placed around a solid structure in front of you.
4. Hold the band at your side in a neutral grip (palms facing your legs).
5. Keep your upper body in good posture throughout the lift.
6. Contract your biceps, pulling the band upwards. As this happens, begin to supinate your forearms.
7. As you pass 90 degrees of elbow flexion, your elbows should come forward slightly to allow a small amount of shoulder flexion.
8. Make a conscious effort to pull your little fingers in towards your chest. This maximises the contraction at the top.
9. Lower under control and don't swing rearwards as you return to the starting position.
10. Complete 3-5 sets of 20 reps.

Massage Ball Biceps Release

This drill uses a massage ball placed against a wall to target specific areas of the arm effectively.

1. Hold a massage ball against a wall with one hand.
2. Keep your other arm straight down to relax your biceps.
3. Push the biceps of the straight arm into the massage ball. At this point, the ball should be supported by the biceps, and you can roll the surrounding muscle mass.
4. Slowly roll up and down the muscle for 30-60 seconds.
5. Perform this 1-2 times on each side.

Barbell Biceps Release Technique

This drill uses the weight of a barbell to release the biceps.

Take caution while performing this drill, and only work with a weight that you can control whilst laying on the floor.

1. Place a barbell on the floor and lay on your side next to it.

2. Extend the lower arm out to your front with your palm facing upwards.

3. Allow your arm to completely relax.

4. Place one sleeve of the barbell onto your biceps.

5. Slowly roll up the barbell sleeve and down the muscle for 30-60 seconds.

6. Don't roll over the crease of your elbow.

7. You can also place the barbell in the groove where your biceps meet your deltoids (shoulders), and from there, slowly flex and extend you elbow 3-5 times.

8. Complete 1-2 times on each side.

Biceps Wall Stretch

This variation of the wall stretch is a great way to get a huge stretch on your biceps.

1. Stand side-on, an arm's distance away from a wall.
2. Place your palm flat to the wall with your fingers facing rearwards.
3. Drive your palm into the wall and turn your biceps downwards without moving the position of your hand.
4. You can gently rotate your body away from your arm to increase the stretch.
5. This stretch can feel incredibly intense as it also targets the median nerve.
6. Hold for 30-60 seconds, or up to 2 minutes if the musculature is very tense.
7. Complete 1-3 times on each side.

Chapter Five: Programming

Introduction

This chapter takes the information from the previous sections and brings it together to create effective programs.

Some are complete back and bicep workouts (*Pull* sessions), while others are specific biceps workouts. Including super-sets (two exercises back-to-back), tri-sets (three exercises back-to-back), or giant-sets (four to six exercises back-to-back).

Most of the rest periods are between 60-90 seconds. However, these can vary when working with heavier loads during compound lifts (up to 2 or 3 minutes), or when performing super-sets.

Pull Workout 1:

Exercise	Sets/Reps/Time	Rest	Notes
Supinated Bent Over Rows	4x10	60-90 Seconds	
Batwing Rows	4x10	60-90 Seconds	
Single Arm Rows	3x20 Each side	60-90 Seconds	
Barbell Curls	4x10	60-90 Seconds	
Incline Dumbbell Curls	4x10	60-90 Seconds	
Hammer Curls	4x10	60-90 Seconds	

Pull Workout 2:

Exercise	Sets/Reps/Time	Rest	Notes
Chin Ups	5x5	60-90 Seconds	
V-Grip Pull Ups	4x3 Each side	60-90 Seconds	
Inverted Rows	4x10	60-90 Seconds	
Drag Curls	4x10	60-90 Seconds	
EZ Bar Preacher Curls	4x10	60-90 Seconds	
Zottman Curls	4x10	60-90 Seconds	

Pull Workout 3:

Exercise	Sets/Reps/Time	Rest	Notes
Supinated Bent Over Rows	4x10	60-90 Seconds	
Inverted Rows	4x10	60-90 Seconds	
Single Arm Rows	3x10 Each side	60-90 Seconds	
Standing EZ Bar Curl	4x10	60-90 Seconds	
Reverse EZ Bar Curls	4x10	60-90 Seconds	
Dumbbell Spider Curls	4x10	60-90 Seconds	

Dumbbell Super-Set:

Complete 3-5 sets of this super-set, with 1-2 minutes rest between sets.

Exercise	Sets/Reps/Time	Rest	Notes
Barbell/EZ Bar Curls	10	3-5 Seconds	
Zottman Curls	10		

Dumbbell Tri-Set:

Complete 3-5 sets of this tri-set, with 1-2 minute rest between sets.

21 Protocol – 7 from bottom to halfway – 7 from halfway to top – 7 from bottom to top.

Exercise	Sets/Reps/Time	Rest	Notes
Cross-Body Hammer Curls	10 Each side	3-5 Seconds	
Hammer Curls	10	3-5 Seconds	
Full Curl 21's	21		

Dumbbell Giant-Set:

Complete 3-5 sets of this giant-set, with 1-2 minute rest between sets.

On the unilateral exercises, alternate the arm you start with.

Exercise	Sets/Reps/Time	Rest	Notes
Drag Curls	10	3-5 Seconds	
Standing EZ Bar Curls	10	3-5 Seconds	
Concentration Curls	10 Each side	3-5 Seconds	
Dumbbell Preacher Curls	10 Each side		

Bonus Content: Fix Your Posture

Introduction

Good movement starts with good posture. However, it's easy to lose the ideal positioning while training. When performing biceps curls, for example, people will often work with shrugged, rounded shoulders and a forward head posture.

Training with poor posture reinforces poor posture, increases the risk of injuries, and often reduces overall performance.

In this section I have added in bonus exercises from my book Fix Your Posture to keep your upper body in good health and optimise the results of your training sessions.

Standing Posture

While standing, the optimal position is to have your feet roughly hip-shoulder width apart, with your knees and hips centred over the middle of your feet halfway between your toes and heels (midfoot).

Your knees should be slightly bent (often referred to as having "soft knees"). This allows the musculature of your legs to help support the surrounding structures while reducing stress on your knees and lower back. Maintaining a soft knee position also allows for better circulation through the legs.

Your torso should be balanced over your hips, not leaning forward or back. Your shoulders should be held back and down, with your chest pushed out and your chin held up and back. This allows your ears to sit directly over the centre of your shoulders, which should in turn align vertically with your hips, knees, and midfoot. These upper body cues should be considered when sitting on a bench.

A great cue for maintaining good posture while standing or walking, is to imagine you are trying to look over a fence that is an inch too high, without going up onto your toes. This will naturally cause you to push your chest out, while retracting your chin and pulling your shoulders back.

Head Retractions & Scapula Pinches

Forward head posture can result in tension headaches and upper back and neck pain.

Head retractions will build a certain degree of strength, especially if resistance is used. However, the main benefit of this exercise is that it helps to build your awareness of proper head positioning. Practise often and it will help to ingrain correct posture.

Head Retractions:

1. Sit upright in your chair.
2. Pull your chin back and slightly up. A tip for getting this right is to place your finger on the vertical groove between your upper lip and nose (your philtrum), push softly and allow your head to retract.
3. Hold the position for 3-5 seconds before releasing.
4. Complete 3-5 sets of 5-10 reps throughout the day.

Scapula Pinches:

Scapula (shoulder blade) pinches are a great exercise. Not only do they free up your upper back, they work to strengthen the muscles which retract your shoulder blades. They can be done while standing or seated.

1. Stand/sit with good posture, relax your shoulders and extend them forward slightly.
2. Pull your shoulders back and concentrate on squeezing your shoulder blades together. Feel your lower traps and rhomboids (muscles between your shoulder blades) scrunch up.
3. Hold the position for 3-5 seconds.
4. Release and slowly bring your shoulders forward.
5. Complete 3-5 sets of 5-10 reps.

Shoulder External Rotation

If someone has a slouched upper body posture with rounded shoulders, their shoulders are often internally rotated. That is, their hands are rotated inwards so that their palms are facing behind them.

The rotator cuff is four deep muscles responsible for stabilising the shoulder joint, as well as both internal and external rotation (rotating the hands back out, so the palms are facing forward). One muscle works as an internal rotator, while the other three work to externally rotate the shoulders.

The internal rotator, along with your chest muscles, often gets plenty of work (due to lots of pushing actions), whereas your external rotators are often underworked, which can result in postural issues.

It's these postural issues that can cause all sorts of problems when you start to bench press and overhead press at the gym. People often say, "The bench press is bad for your shoulders…" but in fact, it's poor posture and poor lifting mechanics/technique on the bench that is bad for your shoulders.

It's vital that we work muscles in ways that specifically target their different roles. The rotator cuff primarily works to stabilise the shoulder joint as it performs various actions. Although facilitating repeated external rotations may not be its main role, all muscles benefit from having their secondary and tertiary actions worked. This exercise will create a deep burn in your shoulders!

The Supraspinatus – One of the rotator cuffs

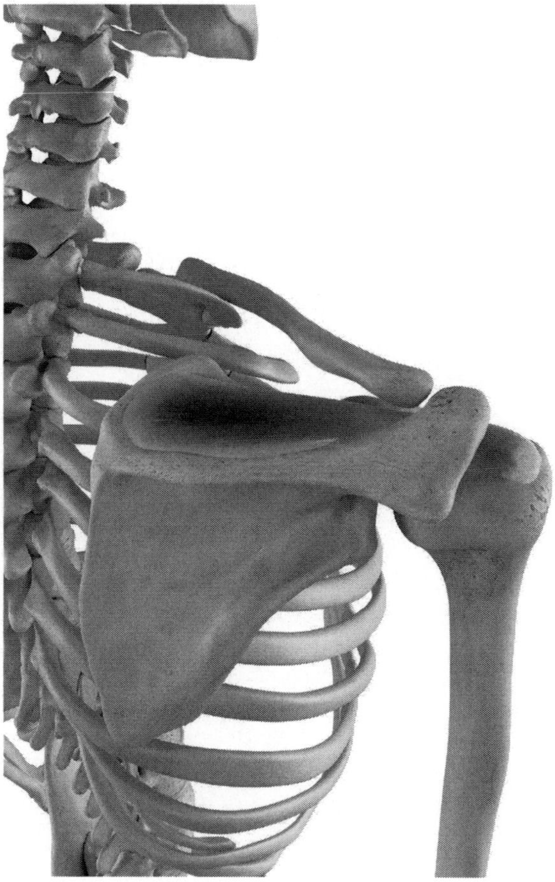

External Rotations - Long Band:

1. Attach a long band to something solid at abdominal height. Use a yellow or red band, increasing tension by standing further from the attachment point if required.
2. Grasp the band with your right hand and turn side-on, so that your left shoulder is closest to the attachment point.
3. Stand with good posture, bend your right elbow to 90 degrees and keep it tucked into your side.
4. Pull the band across your body while externally rotating your right shoulder. Ensure your body stays forward facing and your right elbow remains tucked into your side.
5. Once you have reached the limit of your range of motion with your elbow tucked in, slowly return to the starting position.
6. Don't allow the band to jerk you back to the starting position. Keep it controlled throughout the whole movement.
7. If your elbow comes away from your side, your large shoulder muscle (delt) will take over, so it's important to hold it close.
8. Complete 2-4 sets of 10 reps on each side.

External Rotations – Small Loop Band:

1. Small loop bands come in varying colours. For this exercise, you will need a low-tension band.

2. Hold the band with both hands. I usually place my thumbs over the band.

3. Bend your elbows at 90 degrees and keep both elbows tucked into your sides.

4. Externally rotate both shoulders at the same time.

5. Don't allow the band to jerk you back to the starting position. Keep it controlled throughout the whole movement.

6. Complete 2-4 sets of 10 reps

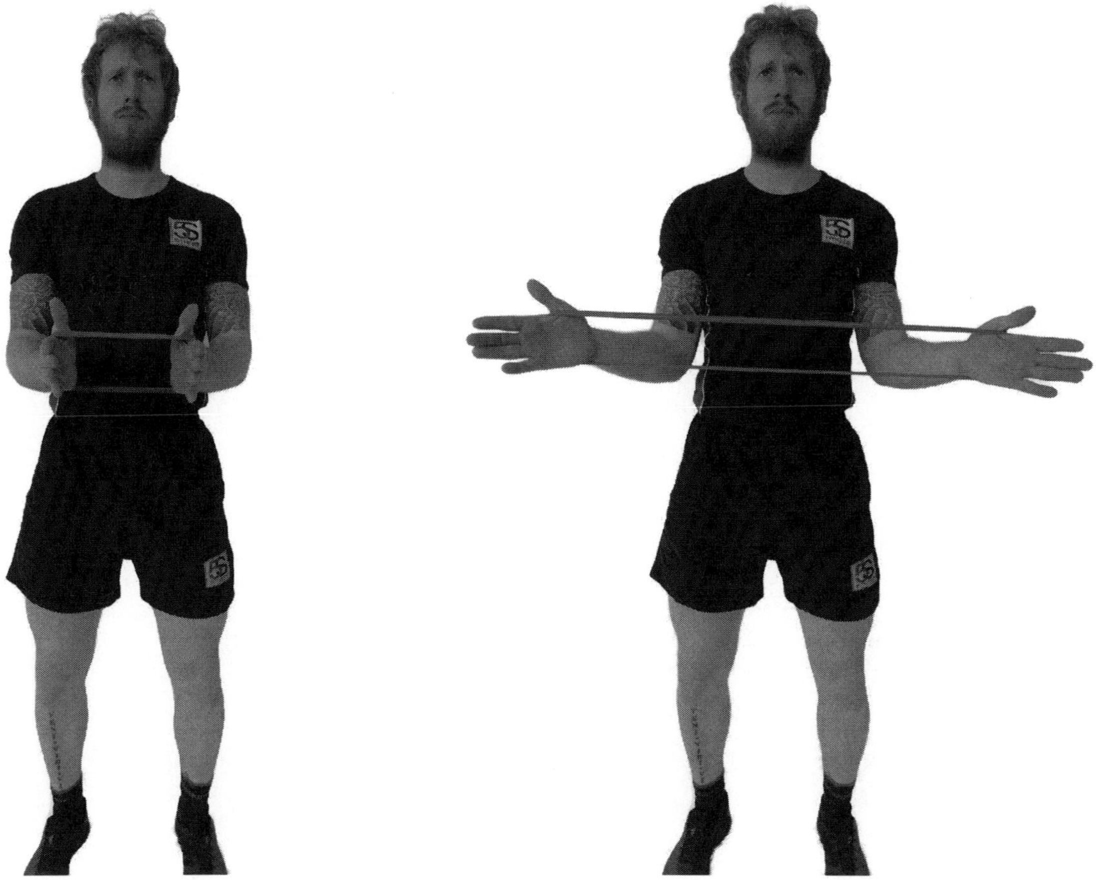

Serratus Wall Slides

Wall slides are a great exercise for your *serratus anterior*, which is often referred to as the "boxer's muscle" due to its job in protracting your shoulders (reaching forward) – an action used when you throw a punch.

The *serratus anterior* muscle originates on the underside of each shoulder blade and wraps around the rib cage (often visible as a jagged muscle on well-trained individuals). These muscles work to pull your shoulder blades flat to your ribcage, while pulling them away from the spine. They aid the upward rotation of your shoulder blades along with your traps.

Upwards rotation is essential for maintaining shoulder health while throwing or pushing your arms overhead. If your shoulder blades don't rotate upwards you're at far greater risk of impingement (rubbing of a tendon) in your shoulders.

If you imagine your shoulder blades being held down while you try to take your arms overhead, you can feel how the motion of the shoulder blades is vital for achieving overhead positions.

The Serratus Anterior

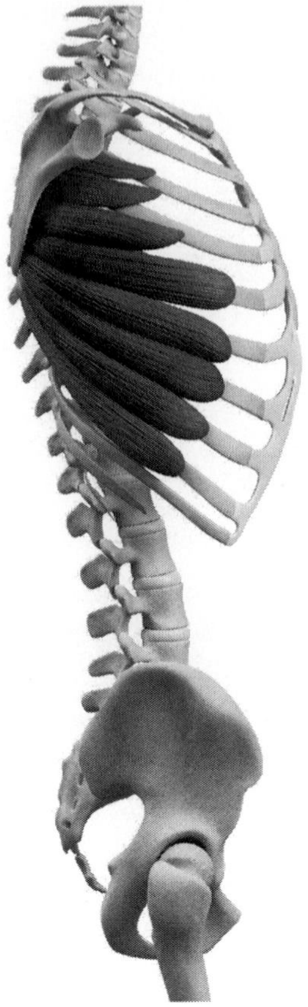

Serratus Wall Slides – Foam Roller:

This exercise uses a foam roller to facilitate the movement smoothly.

1. Place the roller against a wall.
2. Facing the wall/foam roller, bend your elbows to 90 degrees and place your forearms on the roller, with the roller just below your wrists.
3. Drive your forearms into the roller as if you are pushing yourself away, extending your shoulders and engaging the *serratus*.
4. Keep your head back and roll the roller up so that your shoulders flex and your elbows start to extend.
5. Feel your *serratus* engage and roll until the roller meets your elbow. Imagine the bottom of your shoulder blades rotating outwards and upwards towards your armpit.
6. Relax as you roll back down to the starting position.
7. Complete 2-4 sets of 5-10 reps.

Band Pull Apart

As a strength and conditioning coach who works with athletes and the general public, I can't overstate how effective band pull apart variations are at restoring and maintaining shoulder health. Every one of the clients I have prescribed these to has had amazing results.

Band pull apart variations are especially great for lifters, but any individual who is looking to restore and maintain good upper-body posture and shoulder health will benefit from them.

During these exercises it's important not to shrug your shoulders and bring your upper traps into play. You want to work the musculature of the upper back that is responsible for shoulder retraction, not elevation.

Standard Pull Apart:

1. Use a yellow or red long band. The tension can be varied by taking a wider or narrower grip.
2. Take an overhand grip (palms facing down) on the band and place your arms out in front of you with your elbows straight. Grip the band at shoulder width if you can.
3. With your arms straight, pull your arms outwards so the band stretches and comes to your mid chest.
4. The band can also be pulled to your abdomen or forehead to vary the angle at which your shoulders are working.
5. Don't allow the band to jerk you back to the starting position. Keep it under control throughout the whole movement.
6. Complete 2-4 sets of 10-20 reps.

Star Pattern:

The star pattern pull apart is a variation which cycles through various pulling positions.

1. Start with the standard pull apart to your mid chest.

2. Pull your right hand downwards and your left arm upwards, so the band comes diagonally across your body.

3. Repeat this action but the opposite way around, right hand upwards and left hand downwards.

4. Repeat the standard pull apart to your upper chest to restart the cycle.

5. Complete 2-4 sets of 10-20 reps (each pull apart = 1 rep).

Extra Drill – Band Front-to-Backs:

The band front-to-back is a great mobility drill for your shoulders that can be practised anytime. I am placing it here with the band pull apart variations as they work well together.

The pull apart works the muscles that retract your shoulders; the front-to-back mobilises all the muscles that restrict shoulder retraction and overhead positions, such as pecs.

1. Grab a red band with a wide overhand grip. The wider your arms, the easier it is to take the band overhead and down towards your glutes.
2. The band allows you the freedom to widen your grip as you pass it overhead. Your grip should be wide enough so that you aren't forced to aggressively stretch the band out as you perform the movement, as this can cause you to shrug your shoulders, engaging musculature rather than promoting mobility.
3. Start with the band at your hips and while maintaining straight arms throughout, pass it overhead until it reaches your glutes, or the range of motion you can achieve.
4. Complete 2-4 sets of 5-10 reps.

Band Face Pulls

Face pulls are one of the best exercises to rehabilitate and develop your upper back and shoulders.

Resistance bands apply "accommodating resistance", so the resistance will increase as you progress through the exercise. This helps to maximise the contraction of the muscles at work. As you get to the top of the face pull, your rear delts, traps and rhomboids are going to have to increase their engagement to overcome the extra resistance as the band tension increases.

1. Use a yellow or red band. You can vary the tension by standing closer or further away from the band attachment point.
2. Attach the band to something solid at chest height, either looping the band around and holding both ends, or looping the band through itself, so you have hold of one end of the band with both hands.
3. Facing the attachment point, grab the band with an overhand grip. You can grasp the band with just your fingers rather than taking a full grip. This will help to encourage the upper back to work as the primary mover rather than the biceps.
4. Step backwards to apply tension to the band.
5. Keep your chin back.
6. Pull backwards and slightly up to bring yourself into a double bicep pose position. Maintain good head posture, pull your hands back to your temples and don't push your head towards the band.
7. Ensure you consciously engage your upper back and rear delts, rather than just pulling with your biceps. Think about the muscle you are working to increase its engagement (mind-muscle connection).
8. Return to the starting position under control, allowing your shoulders to extend slightly.
9. Complete 2-4 sets of 10-20 reps.

Band Horizontal Pulls

Horizontal pulling actions can be done well on cable/resistance machines. However, bands are more accessible and have the added benefit of accommodating resistance.

I recommend you incorporate horizontal pulling exercises as much as you can. It's commonly recommended for those who train often to incorporate 2-3 times more pulling than pushing.

Bilateral:

Bilateral refers to using both sides of your body at the same time. This exercise can be done while standing or sitting.

1. Use a red or higher tension band. The tension can be varied by standing closer or further away from the band attachment point.
2. Attach the band to something solid at abdominal/lower chest height. Facing the attachment point, grab each end of the band with a neutral grip.
3. Walk backwards to apply tension to the band.
4. Pull the band to your sides, ensuring you consciously engage your back muscles, rather than just pulling with your biceps (mind-muscle connection).
5. Ensure you really concentrate on retracting your shoulders
6. Return to the starting position under control, allowing your shoulders to protract slightly.
7. Complete 2-4 sets of 10-20 reps.

Unilateral:

The unilateral pull involves the same set up as the bilateral pull, but both ends of the band are held in one hand.

The unilateral pull works as a great anti-rotation exercise (discussed in more detail in chapter six). This is essentially a core exercise which works the muscles that resist rotational forces on your spine, which are integral for injury prevention.

Glossary of Terms and Equipment

Anatomical Term	Definition/Description
Abdominals Rectus Abdominis / Obliques	Muscles on the front of the abdomen – rectus abdominis (6 pack muscles) / obliques (muscles to the side of the rectus abdominis).
Achilles Tendon	Tendon on the back of the heel.
Adductors	Muscles on the inner side of the thighs.
Calves Gastrocnemius / Soleus	Muscles on the rear of the lower leg.
Core Musculature	The musculature of your torso, but more specifically it is the lumbo-pelvic region (lumbar spine and pelvis, often referred to as your 'lower back'). These muscles are responsible for both stabilisation and the transfer of force from one of movement to the next, for example changing direction.
Deltoid (delts)	Shoulder muscles – anterior delts (front section) / medial delts (middle section) / posterior delts (rear section).
Diaphragm	A dome shaped muscle used in respiration.
Erector Spinae	Muscles that run up either side of the spine
Gluteals (Glutes) Maximus / Medius / Minor	The buttock muscles – major (largest muscle) / medius (middle muscle) / minor (smallest muscle). The gluteal muscles along with the TFL are also referred to as the hip abductors.
Hamstrings Biceps Femoris / Semimembranosus / Semitendinosus	The three muscles on the rear side of the upper leg
Hip Flexors Psoas Major / Iliacus	The muscles on the front of the hips.
Iliotibial Band (ITB)	A band of connective tissue that runs down the outer side of the thigh.
Latissimus Dorsi (Lats)	Mid- back muscle.
Ligaments	A short band of tough, flexible fibrous connective tissue which connects two bones, and helps to hold a joint together.
Muscle Insertion	The insertion is where the muscle ends and is the point at which the muscle is attached to the bone moved by that muscle.
Muscle Origin	The origin is the start of a muscle and is attached to the fixed bone, which is the one which doesn't move during the contraction.
Pectoralis (Pecs) Major / Minor	Chest muscles – major (larger muscle) / minor (smaller muscle)
Peroneals Peroneus Longus / Peroneus Brevis	Muscles on the outer side of the lower legs.
Piriformis	Small muscle underneath the gluteus maximus.
Plantar Fascia	Thick band of connective tissue on the sole of the foot.

Quadratus Lumborum (QL)	Muscles on either side of the lower back.
Quadriceps (Quads) Rectus Femoris / Vastus Medialis / Vastus Intermedius / Vastus Lateralis	The four muscles of the thigh.
Rhomboids	Upper back muscles between the shoulder blades.
Sciatic Nerve	A major nerve extending from the lower end of the spinal cord, through the glutes and down the back of the thigh.
Tendons	A flexible but inelastic cord of strong fibrous collagen tissue attaching a muscle to a bone.
Tensor Fasciae Latae (TFL)	Muscle on the upper outer side of the thigh.
Thoracic Spine	The thoracic spine is the twelve vertebrae between the base of your neck and the bottom of your rib cage. Often when we refer to the thoracic spine in a training environment, we are referring to the muscles which surround it.
Transverse Abdominis (TVA)	The deepest muscle of the abdominal wall and is an integral component of the core
Trapezius (Traps)	Upper back muscle.

Technical Term	Definition/Description
1 Rep Max (1RM)	Most you can lift for 1 rep. I usually work off *Training Maxes*, meaning there is no breakdown in form.
Abduction	Moving limbs back in towards the midline from a lateral position.
Activation	Getting a specific muscle working.
Adduction	Moving a limb laterally away from the midline.
Agonist	The muscle performing the action – the biceps during a biceps curl.
Anatomical Breathing	Synchronizing your breathing with your movements
Antagonist	The muscles that produce an opposing joint torque to the agonist muscles – the triceps during a biceps curl.
Anterior	Front of the body.
Anterior Pelvic Tilt	Pelvis that tilts excessively forward.
Anti-Extension	Resisting forces that try to extend your spine.
Anti-flexion/Lateral Flexion	Resisting forces that try to flex or laterally-flex your spine.
Anti-Rotation	Resisting forces that try to rotate your spine.
Assistance Lifts	Often referred to as *accessory exercises* are also compound movements. They are chosen to develop specific movements or muscle groups that help you to perform the primary lift or specific sporting actions.
Auxiliary Lifts	These single joint exercises. They are chosen to help develop your ability to perform the primary lift or specific sporting actions.
Ballistic	Refers to movements that exhibit maximum acceleration and velocity over short periods of time. Essentially both the concentric (upwards) and eccentric (downwards) phases of this lift are completed with good speed.
Bilateral	Working both sides of the body at the same time.
Biomechanical breathing	Breathing in before or during the eccentric phase, and breathing out during the later stages or after the concentric phase. This method increases total body tension.
Cadence	Stride frequency – the number of strides a runner takes in a minute.
Cervical Spine	Neck – should have a normal lordotic/inwards curve (lordosis).
Compound Exercises/ Movements	Exercises which include multiple joints and muscle groups.
Concentric Phase/Contraction	The upwards phase of a movement, where the muscle(s) are shortening under tension.
Delayed Onset Muscle Soreness (DOMS)	The muscle soreness you feel days after a workout.
Diaphragmatic Breathing	Effectively using the diaphragm during respiration.
Dorsi-Flexion	Refers to flexion at your ankle so that your toes are pointing upwards
Dynamic Effort Method	Lifting at speed – Working between 50-60% of 1RM.
Eccentric Phase/Contraction	The downwards phase of a movement, where the muscle(s) are lengthening under tension.
Extension	when the angle between the two bones increases – straightening a joint.

Fixators & Neutralizers	These muscles help to stabilize the movement.
Flexibility	This refers to a range of motion a muscle can achieve passively, essentially the length it can achieve.
Flexion	When the angle decreases between the two bones attached to either side of the joint being affected – bending a joint.
Foot Strike	The way the foot lands while running.
Golgi Tendon Organ	Receptor organ that senses changes in muscle tension. It can tell muscles to *shut off* when stimulated.
Intra-abdominal Pressure (IAP)	Increased pressure in the abdomen caused by a held breath and contraction of the core muscles.
Isometric Contraction	A muscle contraction where there is no change in muscle length
Lateral-Flexion	Side bending of the spine.
Low Back Pain	Pain, muscle tension, or stiffness localized below the costal margin (bottom rib) and above the inferior gluteal folds (bottom of your buttocks), with or without sciatica.
Lumbar Spine	Lower back – should have a normal lordotic/inwards curve (lordosis).
Lumbo-Pelvic Region	The lumbar spine and pelvis.
Maximal Effort Training	Maximal weight. Working above 90% of your 1RM
Midline	Centre line of the body
Mind-Muscle Connection (MMC)	Consciously thinking about the muscle, you are working to increase its engagement.
Mobility	How freely a joint can move throughout its full range of motion actively. Flexibility is one very important aspect of mobility.
Motor Unit	A neuron and the muscle fibres which it contracts.
Muscle Tension	Tension is often considered to be the same as tightness. However, not only tight or overworked muscles become tense. Muscles that are lengthened or weak can also become tense – examples of these will pop up throughout the book.
Muscle Tightness	This refers to the muscle-length. If a muscle is tight, then it is shortened. Some muscles have the tendency to be shorter and tighter, while others have the tendency to be longer and less activated.
Muscular Imbalance	Occurs when opposing muscles provide different directions of tension due to tightness and/or weakness.
Nasal Breathing	Breathing through the nose.
Negative Stress	Physical Stress that is maladaptive and leads to injuries and regressions in physical performance.
Neutral Pelvis	A pelvis which sits in the optimal position.
Neutral Spine	A spine which is unbent and untwisted, with three natural curves.
Over-Pronation	When your soles turn outwards slightly more than what is considered optimal, placing more load onto the inner side of the ball of your foot.
Plantar-Flexion	Refers to extension at your ankle so that your toes point downwards towards the floor.

Positive Stress	Physical stress that is adaptive and leads to improvements in physical performance.
Posterior	Rear of the body.
Posterior Pelvic Tilt	Pelvis that tilts excessively rearwards.
Posture	A position which aligns your body so that minimal stress is placed on joints and the supporting muscles, tendons, and ligaments. This results in the stresses of daily life being distributed evenly.
Potentiate/Post-Activation Potentiation (PAP)	Potentiation in this context refers to the increase of strength in nerve pathways that have been used previously. Which in layman's terms, means that the associated muscles are primed and working at full capacity. We can use PAP to capitalise on an increase in neuromuscular efficiency – lighter loads often feel abnormally light after working with heavier loads.
Primary Lift	These are compound exercises. They are of most importance in terms of exercise selection as they work movements fully and require the most effort. Therefore, they should be trained first.
Primary/Prime Mover	The muscle most responsible for completing an action.
Pronated Grip	Overhand Grip.
Pronation/Eversion of the Foot	This refers to when the weight it shifted to the inner side of the foot (soles facing outwards).
Proprioception	The body's ability to transmit a sense of position, analyze that information and react to it.
Protraction	Forward movements of structures of the body.
RAMP	A warmup protocol – refers to *Raise, Activate, Mobilise, Potentiate*.
Range of Motion (ROM)	The full movement potential of a joint.
Release Techniques/ Myofascial Release	A method of hands-on therapy that you can perform yourself, usually with a foam roller or massage ball.
Repeated Effort Method	Submaximal weight for maximal reps – I usually program between 60-75% for this method.
Reps & Sets	*Reps* (repetitions) define the number of times you complete an exercise, and *sets* refers to how many times you will repeat that exercise for the specified number of reps. For example, 5 sets of 3 reps (5x3 – sets first), with 2 minute's rest between sets.
Retraction	Rearwards movements of structures of the body.
Sacrum & Coccyx	Back of the pelvis.
Secondary & Tertiary Movers.	Terms used to describe muscles which assist the prime mover (2nd and 3rd to). During compound lifts, often muscles that may not be considered the prime mover, might be producing just as much force to complete the action.
Single-Joint Exercises	Exercises which work a single joint to target a specific muscle.
Strength	Strength is your ability to produce force, the more force you can produce to overcome a resistance (usually tested with a single effort), the stronger you are.
Submaximal Effort Training	Submaximal weight for submaximal reps. Working between 70-90% of 1RM – I usually program between 75-85% of 1RM.
Supinated Grip	Underhand Grip.

Supination/Eversion of the Foot	This refers to when the weight is shifted to the outer side of the foot (soles facing inwards).
Synergists	The muscle(s) which assist the prime mover.
Thoracic Spine	Mid-upper back – should have a normal kyphotic/outwards curve (kyphosis).
Total Body Tension	Creating tension throughout the body by contracting muscles, using the valsalva maneuver and capitalizing on intra-abdominal pressure.
Training Density	The work you can do in each amount of time. For example, 5x10 reps in 15 minutes is less density that 10x10 reps in 15 minutes.
Training Frequency	How often you train.
Training Intensity	How hard you train. For example, how heavy you lift, or how fast you run.
Training Volume	How much you do in a session/workout.
Unilateral	Working one side of the body at a time.
Valsalva Maneuver	A moderately forceful attempted exhalation against a closed airway. Like equalizing your ears on an airplane and blowing against a pinched nose.

Equipment	Definition/Description
Barbell	The barbell is a 7ft long straight bar that weighs 20kg (44lb) and can have weight plates attached to either side. Lower weight bars are available in some gyms.
Dumbbells	Dumbbells are a short bar with a weight (*bell*) at each end. Most gyms will have a wide selection of dumbbells in 1-2.5kg (2-5lb) increments.
Foam Roller	A 90cm foam roller is ideal, (30-45cm rollers are also fine). However, if you choose to spend more you can purchase a 'rumble roller' which allows you to get deeper into specific areas.
Kettlebell	A kettlebell is a large cast-iron ball-shaped weight with a single handle known as the *horn*. Kettlebells usually come in 4kg (9lb) increments.
Massage Ball	You can purchase balls designed specifically for massage, or use a lacrosse ball. Golf balls can be used (rolling the sole of the foot), but they're often too small to be truly effective. Peanut-shaped massage balls allow you to work both sides of your back, while avoiding pressure on your spine.
Plyo Box or Fitness Step	Strength & Conditioning gyms will usually have wooden plyo boxes which allow for three heights to be used (20/24/30 inch), and jerk boxes which stack various box heights. Most commercial gyms will have some form of plyo box, or fitness steps.
Resistance Bands	Long resistance bands come in varying colours, which denote the tension of the band. Yellow: Low tension Red: Medium tension (recommended) Black: Medium tension (greater tension than red)
Small Loop Resistance Bands	Small bands are a great tool for hip and shoulder strengthening drills. The colours of these bands denote varying band tension. However, these colours can vary and therefore, I advise buying a set of 4-5 bands of varying tensions.

Printed in Great Britain
by Amazon

54106606R00041